Vegan Air Fryer Cookbook for Beginners 2019-2020

5-Ingredient Affordable, Quick & Healthy Budget Friendly Recipes | Heal Your Body, Regain Confidence & Live A Healthy lifestyle | 21-Day Meal Plan

Barben Jamsen

By reading this document, the reader agrees that under no circumstances are we responsible for any losses, direct or indirect, which are incurred as a result of the use of information contained within this document, including, but not limited to, errors, omissions, or inaccuracies.

Table of contents

Introduction

What do French fries, buffalo cauliflower, falafel, and corn fritters have in common? They're vegan, delicious, and often fried in boatloads of oil to achieve that crisp, mouthwatering exterior.

Thus, if you're someone who wants to live healthier, you probably only eat fried food on your cheat days.

Even then, it's understandable to feel guilty because you know that what you're eating is not exactly what you'd call healthy.

Traditional frying can also be quite messy with all the splatters and grease build up, which makes cleaning such a chore.

It is for these reasons why air fryers have become very popular over the last couple of years.

In this day and age where everyone is conscious about their health, air frying is a welcome innovation.

Imagine being able to eat all the fried foods you want without worry!

However, before you go out and get yourself an air fryer to make potato wedges, you need to understand that consuming too much of anything has consequences.

This is true even of air fried foods because similar to their traditionally cooked counterparts, they are still fried.

And while air-fried foods generally contain less fat, eating too much on a regular basis can lead to increased overall consumption of calories, which can cause weight gain.
So, remember: everything in moderation.

If you want to know more about air fryers, this book gives you the basics.

You'll learn the benefits of using an air fryer compared to other kitchen appliances, how you can use an air fryer, as well as how to clean and maintain it so it lasts a long time. You'll also get the nitty gritty of the vegan diet, why it's beneficial and what it can do for your health.

On top of all these, you'll also be happy to know that you'll be getting plenty vegan recipes that you can prepare using the air fryer.

This spells ultimate convenience for you.

Are you ready to get started?

Chapter 1: Air Fryer 101

What is an Air Fryer?

A kitchen appliance that's been around since 2010, an air fryer is like a small, countertop version of a convection oven. It cooks food by circulating hot air around the food with the help of a mechanical fan. Despite its name, an air fryer not only "fries" food. It can also be used to roast vegetables and even bake vegan cookies and cakes.

Advantages of Using an Air Fryer

For most people, the air fryer is one of the best things that happened to healthy eating because it allows you to enjoy your favorite fried foods without the guilt. However, there are other advantages to having this appliance in your kitchen.

1. Frying without massive amounts of oil

Obviously, the biggest benefit you can get out of an air fryer is the fact that you can fry foods without having to use a lot of oil. And compared to using an oven to make baked fries, fries made in an air fryer are crispier without being dried out.

2. No-fuss cooking

Apart from knowing the basics of what you can and can't cook, an air fryer is simple and easy to use. Once you've selected the temperature and cooking time, all you need to do is shake the food around several times during the cooking process.

3. Meals that take less time to prepare

While a conventional oven needs around 30 minutes to pre-heat before you can start cooking your food, an air fryer only takes a few minutes. Air frying also takes significantly less time to cook food and some air fryers even come with baskets that have several compartments so you can cook different foods at the same time.

4. Multiple uses

As mentioned, an air fryer does more than just cook fried foods. It can also be used for baking, grilling, broiling, and stir-frying. In addition, it can be used to cook frozen food without the need to thaw it beforehand.

5. Energy savings

If you've used your oven on the hottest day in summer, you know how it can easily heat up the kitchen and even the rest of the house. You won't have this problem with an air fryer.

6. Easy clean up

Using an air fryer is not the only easy part. Clean up is simple as well because all you need to wash are the basket, tray, and pan. If the components are dishwasher safe, then your job is done.

7. Ideal even for small spaces

Air fryers are generally compact so they can easily be stored on the counter or in the cupboards. Moreover, not all kitchens have enough space for a proper oven, such as dorms, tiny houses, or RVs so an air fryer can really come in handy.

How it Works

Like convection ovens, air fryers cook food with the use of dry heat. It is typically composed of a heating mechanism as well as a fan to circulate the hot air around the food. The rapid air circulation is what makes food crisp and tasty.

Moreover, the basket where the food is placed has holes, which allow the heated air to pass around the food. The basket itself helps intensify the heat inside the air fryer so cooking time is significantly lower than if you would cook the same food in the oven.

How to Start Cooking in an Air Fryer

Air fryers typically have the same components but using the appliance can vary depending on the brand as well as the model. This is why becoming familiar with the user manual is essential before you start using your air fryer.

Cooking with an air fryer can seem daunting if you're using it for the first time so it's helpful to keep in mind these three steps: getting the food ready, getting the appliance ready, and the cooking proper.

In the first step of preparing the food, be sure to cut the ingredients in equal portions for even cooking. Dry the food as well as possible, (optional) spray or wipe a bit of oil on the basket to keep food from sticking and, arrange the food in the basket with adequate space in between.

The next step is to prep the air fryer itself. Like a traditional oven, it needs to preheat before cooking, but instead of taking 20 minutes or so, turning on the appliance and keeping it about 5 minutes is enough. Once adequately heated, the air fryer is ready to use.

Then, you're ready to cook. Place the basket in the air fryer and cook according to the recipe. If you're frying vegetable sticks or wedges, be sure to shake the fryer several times during cooking for even browning. Don't worry about opening the air fryer while cooking because it wouldn't lose heat like opening a convection oven would.

How to Clean and Maintain Your Air Fryer

Cleaning the air fryer is necessary after every use to ensure that flavors from the food you just cooked won't transfer to the next. The basket, pan, and tray are usually dishwasher safe and if there are hard to remove stains, just soak in warm, soapy water for a few minutes. Then, use a damp cloth to clean the inside as well as the outside of the air fryer. Allow the inside components to dry completely before placing them back in the appliance.

When cleaning the air fryer, don't use metal utensils when removing food particles that have gotten stuck on the appliance because this can chip the non-stick coating. If you notice any unpleasant odors, use a paste of baking soda and water to clean the fryer as well as get rid of the smells.

As with any machine, regular maintenance is essential to keep the air fryer in good working condition. Doing so is even more important if you seldom use the air fryer. Periodic maintenance includes:

- Taking care that no food is left behind in the air fryer
- Ensuring that the inside of the air fryer is free from foreign debris
- Checking that the basket, pan, tray, and other components are free from damage
- Checking for frayed or damaged cord
- Taking care not to place the appliance in an enclosed space while in use
- Properly storing the air fryer when not in use

Chapter 2: Vegan Basics

What is Vegan?

Contrary to popular belief, vegan is not simply a type of diet.

It is actually a lifestyle that involves abstinence from the use of any animal products, not just food but any other product made from animal-derived materials (e.g. bags made from crocodile skin, jackets made of bear's fur and so on).

In this book, we will focus primarily on vegan diet, which is often confused with vegetarian diet.

In a vegetarian diet, the dieter consumes primarily fruits and vegetables and completely avoids meat, fish, seafood and poultry. However, the difference between vegans and vegetarians is that the latter still consumes animal derived products that are non-meat such as eggs, honey, milk and dairy. Vegans do not consume anything that is made of or by animals.

Why We Eat Vegan

Vegans have various reasons for adopting this type of diet.
Many do for health reasons.

In a report by the Academy of Nutrition and Diabetics, it has been shown that vegans are at less risk of many serious health conditions including cancer, heart disease, diabetes and high blood pressure, among others.

Research has also proven that vegans on average weigh 20 pounds lighter than people who consume meat. But unlike weight loss fad diets, this one produces long-term results and does not leave you feeling sluggish and weak.

Other vegans do this to save animals. Going vegan actually helps save up to 200 animals each year. This not only reduces the number of deaths but also prevents major sufferings in animal farms. Choosing plant-based food products is definitely the way to go for many animal lovers.

Guidelines and Rules for Eating Vegan

There are actually different types of vegan diets that you have to know about, and right away, you'll get the guidelines and rules for each one. They are quite simple and straightforward.

- Whole food vegan diet

This vegan diet focuses on the consumption of whole plant foods including whole grains, legumes, nuts, seeds, fruits and vegetables.

- Raw food vegan diet

This one involves eating fruits and vegetables and other plant foods that are raw and fresh, or are cooked at temperatures below 118 degrees F.

- 80/10/10 vegan diet

In this type of vegan diet, you will have to limit intake of plants that are rich in fat such as nuts, avocados, and so on. Instead, you will consume mainly fresh raw fruits and leafy greens.

- Starch solution vegan diet

This refers to a low-fat, high-carb vegan diet that focuses on consumption of cooked starches such as rice, corn and potatoes.

- Junk food vegan diet

In this type of diet, the person eats mock meats and mock cheeses, vegan desserts and other processed vegan foods.

It depends on you which one you should follow but basically, it would be a good idea to eat a balanced vegan diet. You can eat processed vegan foods occasionally but make sure that you also eat whole plant foods and fresh raw fruits.

What to Eat

Here's a list of the foods that you can eat:

- Fruits and vegetables
- Tofu, tempeh, seitan
- Legumes (beans, lentils, peas)
- Nuts and nut butters
- Seeds (hemp, chia, flaxseeds, sunflower seeds)
- Vegan milks and yogurts
- Nutritional yeast
- Whole grains, cereals
- Plant foods (miso, kimchi, pickles, kombucha)
- Mushrooms
- Non-dairy milk (almond milk, soy milk, coconut milk)

Basically, anything derived from plants can be consumed in a vegan diet as long as edible and healthy. You can also eat food products designed for vegan diet (vegan butter, vegan cheese, and so on).

What Not to Eat

Here's a list of foods that you cannot eat:

- Meat (beef, lamb, pork, organ meat, horse, veal)
- Poultry (chicken, turkey, duck, quail, goose)
- Fish and seafood
- Dairy (milk, yogurt, cheese, butter, cream, ice cream)
- Eggs
- Any bee product
- Any product with animal-based ingredients (egg whites, whey, lactose, casein, gelatin)

Remember, if the food product is from animal or created by animals, you cannot consume it if you're a vegan.

Tips for Success

Going vegan is not that easy. But here are tips on how you can achieve success with it:

Tip # 1 – Go slow

It may not be easy to suddenly shift to a meatless diet. Vegan is quite restrictive that you may find it difficult to adopt this diet at first. Don't worry. You can start gradually. You can start by first eliminating meat and meat products from your diet. Once you get used to it, then you can start avoiding other animal-derived products such as eggs, dairy and so on.

Tip # 2 – Don't succumb to pressures from people around you

People around you may not understand your decision to go vegan.

But you don't have to worry about what they think or what they say because this is your body, so it's ultimately your decision.

Also, you have to keep in mind that you're not doing anything bad, and that vegan diet is actually beneficial for your health.

Tip # 3 – Plan your meals

It helps to plan your meals by creating a weekly menu and listing down all the ingredients that you'll need to prepare these dishes.

Choose those that are easy and quick to prepare especially during times when you're busy so that you won't get tempted to go back to your old meat-eating ways.

Tip # 4 – Plan dining out

Eating at restaurants and at parties can be a challenge for any vegan.

Before going to a specific restaurant, check out if the menu has options for vegans. Go to restaurants that do have vegan menu selections.

If you are invited to a party, let your friend know that you have adopted a vegan lifestyle and that you will appreciate it if there are vegan foods that can be served for you.

Tip # 5 – Consider taking supplements

Going on a vegan diet may mean missing out on certain key nutrients that the body needs to thrive and be healthy. One example is vitamin B12.

Consider taking a supplement for this vitamin so that you do not end up becoming vitamin B12 deficient.

Be sure to consult your doctor first before taking any supplement.

Chapter 3: 21-Day Meal plan

Day 1

Breakfast: Scrambled Vegan Eggs and Fruits

Lunch: Avocado Rolls

Dinner: Cauliflower Steak

Day 2

Breakfast: Breakfast Burrito

Lunch: Buffalo Cauliflower

Dinner: Lasagna

Day 3

Breakfast: Vegan Omelet and Avocado Slices

Lunch: Seitan Riblets

Dinner: Roasted Vegetable Salad

Day 4

Breakfast: Breakfast Vegan Smoothie

Lunch: Black Bean Burger

Dinner: "Crab" Cake

Day 5

Breakfast: Breakfast Burrito

Lunch: Fried Ravioli

Dinner: Sweet & Spicy Cauliflower

Day 6

Breakfast: French Toast

Lunch: Chickpea Tacos

Dinner: Italian Tofu

Day 7

Breakfast: "Bacon" Breakfast

Lunch: Lentil Balls with Rice

Dinner: Vegetable and Pasta Salad

Day 8

Breakfast: Breakfast Tofu Scramble

Lunch: Barbecue Soy Curls

Dinner: Buffalo Cauliflower

Day 9

Breakfast: Breakfast Burrito

Lunch: Falafel

Dinner: Roasted Vegetable Salad

Day 10

Breakfast: Breakfast Frittata

Lunch: Lemon Tofu

Dinner: Mushroom and Green Bean Casserole

Day 11

Breakfast: Fruit Crumble

Lunch: Roasted Vegetable Salad

Dinner: Tofu Buddha Bowl

Day 12

Breakfast: Strawberry Smoothie

Lunch: Crispy Vegetables

Dinner: Lentil Balls with Rice

Day 13

Breakfast: Breakfast Potatoes

Lunch: Eggplant Parmesan

Dinner: Roasted Spicy Carrots

Day 14

Breakfast: Oats, Almond Milk and Fruits

Lunch: Crispy Zucchini Wedges

Dinner: Barbecue Soy Curls

Day 15

Breakfast: Quinoa Topped With Berries

Lunch: Crispy Tofu and Avocado Salad

Dinner: Italian Tofu

Day 16

Breakfast: Tofu & "Sausage" Sandwich

Lunch: Eggplant Parmesan

Dinner: Vegetable and Pasta Salad

Day 17

Breakfast: Breakfast Casserole

Lunch: Lentil Balls with Rice

Dinner: Chickpea Tacos

Day 18

Breakfast: Vegan Pancakes

Lunch: Cauliflower Steak

Dinner: Salad with Roasted Tomatoes

Day 19

Breakfast: Breakfast Sandwich

Lunch: Tofu Buddha Bowl

Dinner: Lasagna

Day 20

Breakfast: Tofu & "Sausage" Sandwich

Lunch: Roasted Butternut Squash Salad

Dinner: Eggplant Parmesan

Day 21

Breakfast: Breakfast Casserole

Lunch: Crispy Tofu and Avocado Salad

Dinner: Crispy Zucchini Wedges

Chapter 4: Breakfast and Brunch Recipes

French Toast

Preparation Time: 5 minutes
Cooking Time: 6 minutes
Servings: 8

Ingredients:

- 1 cup pecans
- 2 tablespoons flaxseeds
- 1 teaspoon ground cinnamon
- 1 cup rolled oats
- ¾ cup almond milk
- 8 pieces whole grain vegan bread
- Maple syrup

Method:

1. Pulse pecans, flaxseeds, cinnamon and oats in the food processor until crumbly.
2. Transfer to a dish.
3. In another place, pour in the almond milk.
4. Soak each bread slice for 10 seconds in the almond milk.
5. Dredge with the pecan mixture.
6. Cook the bread in the air fryer at 350 degrees for 3 minutes.
7. Flip the bread and cook for an additional 3 minutes.
8. Drizzle maple syrup on top.

Nutritional Value:

- Calories 308
- Total Fat 27.6g
- Saturated Fat 6.7g
- Cholesterol 0mg
- Sodium 113mg
- Total Carbohydrate 14.4g
- Dietary Fiber 4.8g
- Total Sugars 3.5g
- Protein 4.9g
- Potassium 237mg

Breakfast Burrito

Preparation Time: 20 minutes
Cooking Time: 8 minutes
Servings: 4

Ingredients:

- 2 tablespoons tamari
- 2 tablespoons cashew butter
- 1 tablespoon water
- 1 tablespoon liquid smoke
- 4 pieces rice paper
- 2 vegan eggs
- ¼ cup sweet potatoes, cubed and roasted
- 8 strips red pepper, roasted
- 6 spears fresh asparagus
- 1 cup kale

Method:

1. In a bowl, mix the tamari, butter, water and liquid smoke.
2. Arrange the rest of the ingredients on top of the rice paper sheets.
3. Roll and seal the ends.
4. Dip each burrito into the tamari mixture.
5. Cook in the air fryer at 350 degrees F for 8 minutes or until crispy.

Nutritional Value:

- Calories 255
- Total Fat 5.2g
- Saturated Fat 0.9g
- Cholesterol 3mg
- Sodium 1553mg
- Total Carbohydrate 39.6g
- Dietary Fiber 5.9g
- Total Sugars 8.2g
- Protein 10.2g
- Potassium 248mg

Breakfast Tofu Scramble

Preparation Time: 5 minutes
Cooking Time: 30 minutes
Servings: 3

Ingredients:

- 1 teaspoon turmeric
- 2 tablespoons soy sauce
- ½ teaspoon onion powder
- ½ teaspoon garlic powder
- ½ cup onion, chopped
- 2 tablespoons olive oil, divided
- 1 block tofu, cubed
- 2 ½ cups potato, cubed

Method:

1. In a bowl, combine the turmeric, soy sauce, onion powder, garlic powder, onion and half of the olive oil.
2. Marinate the tofu cubes in the mixture for 10 minutes.
3. In another bowl, coat the potato cubes with the remaining olive oil.
4. Cook the potatoes in the air fryer at 400 degrees F for 15 minutes, shaking halfway through.
5. Add the tofu and cook at 370 degrees F for another 15 minutes.

Nutritional Value:

- Calories 168
- Total Fat 10.7g
- Saturated Fat 1.6g
- Cholesterol 0mg
- Sodium 610mg

- Total Carbohydrate 15.2g
- Dietary Fiber 2.4g
- Total Sugars 1.9g
- Protein 4.8g
- Potassium 387mg

Fruit Crumble

Preparation Time: 15 minutes
Cooking Time: 15 minutes
Servings: 2

Ingredients:

- 1 apple, diced
- ¼ cup frozen strawberries
- ¼ cup frozen blueberries
- 2 tablespoons sugar
- ¼ cup brown rice flour
- 2 tablespoons vegan butter
- ½ teaspoon ground cinnamon

Method:

1. Preheat your air fryer to 350 degrees F for 5 minutes.
2. In a ramekin, combine the apple, strawberries and blueberries.
3. In a bowl, mix the rest of the ingredients.
4. Pour the mixture over the fruits and mix well.
5. Cook in the air fryer at 350 degrees F for 15 minutes.

Nutritional Value:

- Calories 310
- Total Fat 12 g
- Saturated Fat 7 g
- Cholesterol 31 mg
- Sodium 5 mg
- Total Carbohydrate 50 g
- Dietary Fiber 5 g
- Total Sugars 26 g
- Protein 2 g
- Potassium 570 mg

Tofu & "Sausage" Sandwich

Preparation Time: 2 minutes
Cooking Time: 13 minutes
Servings: 2

Ingredients:

- 2 vegan bagels, sliced in half
- 2 vegan breakfast sausages
- ½ teaspoon oil
- 4 thin slices tofu
- Salt and pepper to taste
- ¼ teaspoon nutritional yeast flakes, divided
- ¼ teaspoon granulated onion, divided
- 2 tablespoons vegan cream cheese

Method:

1. Toast the bagels in your toaster until golden.
2. Set aside.
3. Air fry the sausages at 400 degrees F for 10 minutes, flipping once halfway through.
4. In a pan over medium heat, add the oil.
5. Sprinkle salt, pepper, nutritional yeast flakes and onion on both sides.
6. Cook the tofu until golden on both sides.
7. Spread cream cheese on the bagel and top with the sausage and tofu.
8. Place the other bagel slice on top.

Nutritional Value:

- Calories 472
- Total Fat 11 g
- Saturated Fat 1 g
- Cholesterol 25 mg
- Sodium 908 mg
- Total Carbohydrate 57 g
- Dietary Fiber 3 g
- Total Sugars 3 g
- Protein 22 g
- Potassium 106 mg

Breakfast Sandwich

Preparation Time: 10 minutes
Cooking Time: 10 minutes
Servings: 4

Ingredients:

- ½ teaspoon turmeric
- 1 teaspoon garlic powder
- ¼ cup light soy sauce
- Paprika to taste
- 4 slices tofu, cut into rounds using cookie cutter
- 4 vegan English muffins, sliced in half
- 4 teaspoons vegan mayonnaise
- 1 avocado, sliced
- 4 slices vegan cheese
- 4 white onion rings
- 4 slices tomato

Method:

1. In a bowl, mix turmeric, garlic powder, soy sauce and paprika.
2. Marinate tofu rounds for 10 minutes.
3. Cook in the air fryer at 400 degrees F for 10 minutes, shaking once halfway through.
4. Spread the mayo on the muffin and put the avocado and cheese on top.
5. Put the tofu above the cheese.
6. Top with onion ring and tomato slice.
7. Place the other half of the muffin on top.

Nutritional Value:

- Calories 226
- Total Fat 7.6g
- Saturated Fat 1.5g
- Cholesterol 0mg
- Sodium 583mg
- Total Carbohydrate 30.6g

- Dietary Fiber 4.2g
- Total Sugars 3.8g

- Protein 11.2g
- Potassium 207mg

Breakfast Casserole

Preparation Time: 10 minutes
Cooking Time: 20 minutes
Servings: 2

Ingredients:

- 1 teaspoon olive oil
- 1 onion, diced
- 1 teaspoon garlic, minced
- ½ cup bell pepper, diced
- ½ cup mushrooms, sliced
- 2 stalks celery, chopped
- 1 carrot, chopped
- Salt and pepper to taste
- ½ teaspoon dried oregano
- ½ teaspoon dried dill
- ½ teaspoon cumin
- 7 oz. tofu
- 2 tablespoons water
- 2 tablespoons soy yogurt
- 2 tablespoons nutritional yeast
- 1 tablespoon lemon juice
- ½ cup cooked quinoa

Method:

1. Pour the olive oil in a pan over medium heat.
2. Cook the onion and garlic for 2 minutes.
3. Add the bell pepper, mushroom, celery and carrot.
4. Season with the salt, pepper, oregano, dill and cumin.
5. Mix well and cook for 3 minutes.
6. In a food processor, put the rest of the ingredients except the quinoa.
7. Pulse until creamy.

8. Pour the mixture into the pan and add the quinoa.
9. Mix well.
10. Transfer the mixture to a baking dish that will fit inside an air fryer.
11. Cook at 350 degrees F for 15 minutes.
12. Let cool a little before serving.

Nutritional Value:

- Calories 352
- Total Fat 10.4g
- Saturated Fat 1.7g
- Cholesterol 0mg
- Sodium 64mg

- Total Carbohydrate 47.8g
- Dietary Fiber 9.6g
- Total Sugars 7.7g
- Protein 21.5g
- Potassium 1000mg

Breakfast Potatoes

Preparation Time: 5 minutes
Cooking Time: 25 minutes
Servings: 4

Ingredients:

- 2 potatoes, chopped
- 2 teaspoons olive oil
- Salt and pepper to taste
- 1 onion, chopped
- 1 bell pepper, chopped

Method:

1. Toss the potatoes in oil and season with salt and pepper.
2. Cook in the air fryer at 400 degrees F for 10 minutes, shaking once halfway through.
3. Add the onion and bell pepper.
4. Toss to mix and cook for 400 degrees for another 10 to 15 minutes.

Nutritional Value:

- Calories 81
- Total Fat 10 g
- Saturated Fat 2 g
- Cholesterol 12 mg
- Sodium 12 mg
- Total Carbohydrate 17 g
- Dietary Fiber 3 g
- Total Sugars 2 g
- Protein 3 g
- Potassium 542 mg

Breakfast Frittata

Preparation Time: 15 minutes
Cooking Time: 20 minutes
Servings: 2

Ingredients:

- Cooking spray
- ¼ lb. breakfast sausage, cooked and crumbled
- 4 vegan eggs
- ½ cup vegan cheese
- 2 tablespoons red bell pepper, diced
- 1 green onion, chopped

Method:

1. Spray oil on a small cake pan.
2. Preheat your air fryer to 360 degrees F.
3. Combine all the ingredients in a bowl.
4. Pour the mixture into the cake pan.
5. Cook in the air fryer for 20 minutes.

Nutritional Value:

- Calories 380
- Total Fat 27 g
- Saturated Fat 12 g
- Cholesterol 443 mg
- Sodium 694 mg
- Total Carbohydrate 3 g
- Dietary Fiber 1 g
- Total Sugars 1 g
- Protein 31.2 g
- Potassium 328 mg

"Bacon" Breakfast

Preparation Time: 15 minutes
Cooking Time: 25 minutes
Servings: 2

Ingredients:

- 2 tablespoons tamari
- 1 tablespoon sesame oil, toasted
- 1 tablespoon olive oil
- 1 teaspoon maple syrup
- 1 teaspoon lemon juice
- 1 teaspoon paprika
- Salt and pepper to taste
- ¼ teaspoon vegan Worcestershire sauce
- ½ teaspoon cumin
- 1 medium eggplant, cut into long thin slices
- 2 tablespoons vegan mayonnaise
- 2 vegan muffins
- 4 tomato slices
- 4 cucumber slices

Method:

1. Preheat your air fryer to 300 degrees F.
2. In a bowl, mix the tamari, oils, maple syrup, lemon juice, paprika, salt, pepper, Worcestershire sauce and cumin.
3. Brush both sides of eggplant slice with the mixture.
4. Arrange the eggplant slices on a single layer on the air fryer pan.
5. Cook for 15 minutes or until brown.
6. Spread mayo on the muffin and put the "bacon" on top.
7. Top with the cucumber and tomato slices.

Nutritional Value:

- Calories 99
- Total Fat 7.2 g
- Saturated Fat 1 g
- Cholesterol 12 mg
- Sodium 748 mg

- Total Carbohydrate 8.9 g
- Dietary Fiber 4.3 g
- Total Sugars 4.7 g
- Protein 1.7 g
- Potassium 297 mg

Chapter 5: Appetizer and Snack Recipes

Veggie Wontons

Preparation Time: 10 minutes
Cooking Time: 15 minutes
Servings: 10

Ingredients:

- Cooking spray
- ½ cup white onion, grated
- ½ cup mushrooms, chopped
- ½ cup carrot, grated
- ¾ cup red pepper, chopped
- ¾ cup cabbage, grated
- 1 tablespoons chili sauce
- 1 teaspoon garlic powder
- Salt and pepper to taste
- 30 vegan wonton wrappers
- Water

Method:

1. Spray oil in a pan.
2. Put the pan over medium heat and cook the onion, mushrooms, carrot, red pepper and cabbage until tender.
3. Stir in the chili sauce, garlic powder, salt and pepper.
4. Let it cool for a few minutes.
5. Add a scoop of the mixture on top of the wrappers.
6. Fold and seal the corners using water.
7. Cook in the air fryer at 320 degrees F for 7 minutes or until golden brown.

Nutritional Value:

- Calories 290
- Total Fat 1.5g
- Saturated Fat 0.3g
- Cholesterol 9mg

- Sodium 593mg
- Total Carbohydrate 58g
- Dietary Fiber 2.3g
- Total Sugars 1.3g
- Protein 9.9g
- Potassium 147mg

Avocado Rolls

Preparation Time: 20 minutes
Cooking Time: 25 minutes
Servings: 5

Ingredients:

- 10 rice paper wrappers
- 3 avocados, sliced
- 1 tomato, diced
- Salt and pepper to taste
- 1 tablespoon olive oil
- 4 tablespoons sriracha
- 2 tablespoons sugar
- 1 tablespoon rice vinegar
- 1 tablespoon sesame oil

Method:

1. Mash avocados in a bowl.
2. Stir in the tomatoes, salt and pepper.
3. Mix well.
4. Arrange the rice paper wrappers.
5. Scoop mixture on top.
6. Roll and seal the edges with water.
7. Cook in the air fryer at 350 degrees F for 5 minutes.
8. Mix the rest of the ingredients.
9. Serve rolls with the sriracha dipping sauce.

Nutritional Value:

- Calories 422
- Saturated Fat 5.8g
- Cholesterol 0mg
- Sodium 180mg
- Total Carbohydrate 38.7g
- Dietary Fiber 8.8g
- Total Sugars 6.5g
- Protein 3.8g
- Potassium 633mg

Fried Ravioli

Preparation Time: 15 minutes
Cooking Time: 8 minutes
Servings: 4

Ingredients:

- ½ cup panko breadcrumbs
- Salt and pepper to taste
- 1 teaspoon garlic powder
- 1 teaspoon dried oregano
- 1 teaspoon dried basil
- 2 teaspoons nutritional yeast flakes
- ¼ cup aquafaba liquid
- 8 oz. frozen vegan ravioli
- Cooking spray
- ½ cup marinara sauce

Method:

1. Mix the breadcrumbs, salt, pepper, garlic powder, oregano, basil and nutritional yeast flakes on a plate.
2. In another bowl, pour the aquafaba liquid.
3. Dip each ravioli into the liquid and then coat with the breadcrumb mixture.
4. Put the ravioli in the air fryer.
5. Spray oil on the raviolis.
6. Cook at 390 degrees F for 6 minutes.
7. Flip each one and cook for another 2 minutes.
8. Serve with marinara sauce.

Nutritional Value:

- Calories 154
- Total Fat 3.8g
- Saturated Fat 0.6g
- Cholesterol 7mg
- Sodium 169mg
- Total Carbohydrate 18.4g
- Dietary Fiber 1.5g
- Total Sugars 3g
- Protein 4.6g
- Potassium 154mg

Corn Fritters

Preparation Time: 15 minutes
Cooking Time: 10 minutes
Servings: 4

Ingredients:

- ¼ cup ground cornmeal
- ¼ cup flour
- Salt and pepper to taste
- ½ teaspoon baking powder
- ¼ teaspoon garlic powder
- ¼ teaspoon onion powder
- ¼ teaspoon paprika
- ¼ cup parsley, chopped
- 1 cup corn kernels mixed with 3 tablespoons almond milk
- 2 cups fresh corn kernels
- 4 tablespoons vegan mayonnaise
- 2 teaspoons grainy mustard

Method:

1. Mix the cornmeal, flour, salt, pepper, baking powder, garlic powder, onion powder, paprika and parsley in a bowl.
2. Put the corn kernels with almond milk in a food processor.
3. Season with salt and pepper.
4. Pulse until well blended.
5. Add the corn kernels.
6. Transfer to a bowl and stir into the cornmeal mixture.
7. Pour a small amount of the batter in the air fryer pan.
8. Pour another a few centimeters away from the first fritter.
9. Cook in the air fryer at 350 degrees for 10 minutes or until golden.
10. Flip halfway through.
11. Serve with mayo mustard dip.

Nutritional Value:

- Calories 135
- Total Fat 4.6g
- Saturated Fat 0.2g
- Cholesterol 0mg
- Sodium 136mg

- Total Carbohydrate 22.5g
- Dietary Fiber 2.5g
- Total Sugars 2.7g
- Protein 3.5g
- Potassium 308mg

Mushroom Pizza

Preparation Time: 15 minutes
Cooking Time: 10 minutes
Servings: 4
Ingredients:

- 4 large Portobello mushrooms, stems and gills removed
- 1 teaspoon balsamic vinegar
- Salt and pepper to taste
- 4 tablespoons vegan pasta sauce
- 1 clove garlic, minced
- 3 oz. zucchini, chopped
- 4 olives, sliced
- 2 tablespoons sweet red pepper, diced
- 1 teaspoon dried basil
- ½ cups hummus
- Fresh basil, minced

Method:

1. Coat the mushrooms with balsamic vinegar and season with salt and pepper.
2. Spread pasta sauce inside each mushroom.
3. Sprinkle with minced garlic.
4. Preheat your air fryer to 330 degrees F.
5. Cook mushrooms for 3 minutes.
6. Take the mushrooms out and top with zucchini, olives, and peppers.
7. Season with salt, pepper and basil.
8. Put them back to the air fryer and cook for another 3 minutes.
9. Serve mushroom pizza with hummus and fresh basil.

Nutritional Value:

- Calories 70
- Total Fat 1.56 g
- Saturated Fat 0.5 g
- Cholesterol 12 mg
- Sodium 167 mg
- Total Carbohydrate 11 g
- Dietary Fiber 3.4 g
- Total Sugars 3.8 g
- Protein 4.3 g
- Potassium 350 mg

Onion Appetizers

Preparation Time: 10 minutes
Cooking Time: 4 minutes
Servings: 4

Ingredients:

- 2 lb. onions, sliced into rings
- 2 vegan eggs
- 1 cup almond milk
- 2 cups flour
- 1 tablespoon paprika
- Salt and pepper to taste
- 1 teaspoon garlic powder
- 1 teaspoon cayenne pepper
- Cooking spray
- ¼ cup vegan mayo
- ¼ cup vegan sour cream
- 1 tablespoon ketchup

Method:

1. Combine the eggs and milk in one plate.
2. In another plate, mix the flour, paprika, salt, pepper, garlic powder and cayenne pepper.
3. Dip each onion into the egg mixture before coating with the flour mixture.
4. Spray with oil.
5. Air fryer at 350 degrees F for 4 minutes or until golden and crispy.
6. Serve with the dipping sauces.

Nutritional Value:

- Calories 364
- Total Fat 14.5g
- Saturated Fat 10.3g
- Cholesterol 0mg
- Sodium 143mg
- Total Carbohydrate 52.7g
- Dietary Fiber 7.2g
- Total Sugars 9.3g
- Protein 8.1g
- Potassium 434mg

Crispy Brussels Sprouts

Preparation Time: 5 minutes
Cooking Time: 1 minutes
Servings: 2

Ingredients:

- 2 cups Brussels sprouts, sliced
- 1 tablespoon olive oil
- 1 tablespoon balsamic vinegar
- Salt to taste

Method:

1. Toss all the ingredients in a bowl.
2. Cook in the air fryer at 400 degrees F for 10 minutes, shake once or twice during the cooking process.
3. Check to see if crispy enough.
4. If not, cook for another 5 minutes.

Nutritional Value:

- Calories 100
- Total Fat 7.3g
- Saturated Fat 1.1g
- Cholesterol 0mg
- Sodium 100mg
- Total Carbohydrate 8.1g
- Dietary Fiber 3.3g
- Total Sugars 1.9g
- Protein 3g
- Potassium 348mg

Sweet Potato Tots

Preparation Time: 10 minutes
Cooking Time: 12 minutes
Servings: 10

Ingredients:

- 2 cups sweet potato puree
- ½ teaspoon salt
- ½ teaspoon cumin
- ½ teaspoon coriander
- ½ cup breadcrumbs
- Cooking spray
- Vegan mayo

Method:

1. Preheat your air fryer to 390 degrees F.
2. Combine all ingredients in a bowl.
3. Form into balls.
4. Arrange on the air fryer pan.
5. Spray with oil.
6. Cook for 6 minutes or until golden.
7. Serve with vegan mayo.

Nutritional Value:

- Calories 77
- Total Fat 0.8g
- Saturated Fat 0.1g
- Cholesterol 0mg
- Sodium 205mg
- Total Carbohydrate 15.9g
- Dietary Fiber 1.1g
- Total Sugars 3.1g
- Protein 1.8g
- Potassium 120mg

Popcorn Tofu

Preparation Time: 15 minutes
Cooking Time: 12 minutes
Servings: 4
Ingredients:

- ½ cup cornmeal
- ½ cup quinoa flour
- 1 tablespoon vegan bouillon
- 2 tablespoons nutritional yeast
- 1 teaspoon garlic powder
- 1 teaspoon onion powder
- 1 tablespoon mustard
- Salt and pepper to taste
- ¾ cup almond milk
- 1 ½ cups breadcrumbs
- 14 oz. tofu, sliced into small pieces
- ½ cup vegan mayo
- 2 tablespoons hot sauce

Method:

1. In the first bowl, mix the first 8 ingredients.
2. In the second bowl, pour the almond milk.
3. In the third bowl, add the breadcrumbs.
4. Dip each tofu slice into each of the bowls starting from the flour mixture, then the almond milk and finally in the breadcrumbs.
5. Cook in the air fryer at 350 degrees F for 12 minutes, shaking halfway through.
6. Mix the mayo and hot sauce and serve with tofu.

Nutritional Value:

- Calories 261
- Total Fat 5.5 g
- Saturated Fat 1 g
- Cholesterol 12 mg
- Sodium 120 mg
- Total Carbohydrate 37.5 g
- Dietary Fiber 4.8 g
- Total Sugars 3 g
- Protein 16 g
- Potassium 430 mg

Black Bean Burger

Preparation Time: 10 minutes
Cooking Time: 25 minutes
Servings: 6

Ingredients:

- 1 ¼ cup rolled oats
- 16 oz. black beans, rinsed and drained
- ¾ cup salsa
- 1 tablespoon soy sauce
- 1 ¼ teaspoons chili powder
- ¼ teaspoon chipotle chili powder
- ½ teaspoon garlic powder

Method:

1. Pulse the oats inside a food processor until powdery.
2. Add all the other ingredients and pulse until well blended.
3. Transfer to a bowl and refrigerate for 15 minutes.
4. Form into burger patties.
5. Cook in the air fryer at 375 degrees F for 15 minutes.

Nutritional Value:

- Calories 158
- Total Fat 2 g
- Saturated Fat 1 g
- Cholesterol 10 mg
- Sodium 690 mg
- Total Carbohydrate 30 g
- Dietary Fiber 9 g
- Total Sugars 2.7 g
- Protein 8 g
- Potassium 351 mg

Chapter 6: Main Dish Recipes

Lemon Tofu

Preparation Time: 15 minutes
Cooking Time: 25 minutes
Servings: 4

Ingredients:

- 1 lb. tofu, sliced into cubes
- 1 tablespoon tamari
- 1 tablespoon arrowroot powder
- ¼ cup lemon juice
- 1 teaspoon lemon zest
- 2 tablespoon sugar
- ½ cup water
- aspoons cornstarch

Method:

1. Coat the tofu cubes in tamari.
2. Dredge with arrowroot powder.
3. Let sit for 15 minutes.
4. Add the rest of the ingredients in a bowl, mix and set aside.
5. Cook the tofu in the air fryer at 390 degrees F for 10 minutes, shaking halfway through.
6. Put the tofu in a skillet over medium high heat.
7. Stir in the sauce.
8. Simmer until the sauce has thickened.
9. Serve with rice or vegetables.

Nutritional Value:

- Calories 112
- Total Fat 3 g
- Saturated Fat 0.5 g
- Cholesterol 10 mg

- Sodium 294 mg
- Total Carbohydrate 13 g
- Dietary Fiber 6 g

- Total Sugars 8 g
- Protein 8 g
- Potassium 250 mg

Buffalo Cauliflower

Preparation Time: 10 minutes
Cooking Time: 12 minutes
Servings: 4

Ingredients:

- 1 cauliflower, sliced into florets
- 2 tablespoons hot sauce
- 1 ½ teaspoons maple syrup
- 2 teaspoons avocado oil
- 2 tablespoons nutritional yeast
- Salt to taste
- 1 tablespoon arrowroot starch

Method:

1. Preheat your fryer to 360 degrees F.
2. In a bowl, put all the ingredients except the cauliflower.
3. Mix well.
4. Toss cauliflower into the mixture to coat evenly.
5. Cook in the air fryer for 14 minutes, shaking halfway during the cooking.

Nutritional Value:

- Calories 52
- Total Fat 0.7g
- Saturated Fat 0.1g
- Cholesterol 0mg
- Sodium 252mg
- Total Carbohydrate 9.5g
- Dietary Fiber 3.1g
- Total Sugars 3.2g
- Protein 3.7g
- Potassium 344mg

Lasagna

Preparation Time: 9 minutes
Cooking Time: 21 minutes
Servings: 1
Ingredients:

- 2 lasagna noodles, broken in half
- Salt to taste
- ½ cup pasta sauce
- ¼ cup vegan cheese
- 1 cup fresh basil, chopped
- ¼ cup baby spinach, chopped
- 1 handful baby spinach leaves chopped, about 1/4 cup chopped
- 3 tablespoons zucchini, shredded

Method:

1. Boil the lasagna noodles according to directions in the package.
2. Drain the noodles.
3. In a loaf pan, spread a tablespoon of the pasta sauce.
4. Top it with the lasagna noodle.
5. Put layers of cheese, basil, spinach and zucchini on top.
6. Add another lasagna noodle and repeat the layers until you've used up all the noodles.
7. Cover the pan with foil.
8. Put inside the air fryer.
9. Cook at 400 degrees F for 10 minutes.
10. Remove the foil.
11. Cook for another 5 minutes.

Nutritional Value:

- Calories 344
- Total Fat 9 g
- Saturated Fat 1 g
- Cholesterol 6 mg
- Sodium 843 mg
- Total Carbohydrate 52 g
- Dietary Fiber 3 g
- Total Sugars 7 g
- Protein 14 g
- Potassium 920 mg

Chickpea Tacos

Preparation Time: 10 minutes
Cooking Time: 20 minutes
Servings: 4

Ingredients:

- 19 oz. canned chickpeas, rinsed and drained
- 4 cups cauliflower florets, chopped
- 2 tablespoons olive oil
- 2 tablespoons taco seasoning
- 4 tortillas
- 4 cups cabbage, shredded
- 2 avocados, sliced
- Soy yogurt

Method:

1. Preheat your air fryer to 390 degrees F.
2. Toss the chickpeas and cauliflower in olive oil.
3. Sprinkle with taco seasoning.
4. Put in the air fryer basket.
5. Cook for 20 minutes, shaking occasionally.
6. Stuff filling into the tortillas and top with cabbage, avocado and yogurt.

Nutritional Value:

- Calories 464
- Total Fat 18.6g
- Saturated Fat 3.2g
- Cholesterol 0mg
- Sodium 363mg
- Total Carbohydrate 61.3g
- Dietary Fiber 18.2g
- Total Sugars 12.8g
- Protein 17.3g
- Potassium 1066mg

Falafel

Preparation Time: 1 hour and 30 minutes
Cooking Time: 10 minutes
Servings: 8

Ingredients:

- ½ cup white onion, chopped
- 7 cloves garlic
- ½ cup fresh cilantro, chopped
- ½ cup fresh parsley, chopped
- 1 ½ cups dry garbanzo beans, soaked in water overnight
- 2 tablespoons all-purpose flour
- 1 tablespoon ground cumin
- 1 teaspoon ground coriander
- ⅛ teaspoon cayenne pepper
- ⅛ teaspoon ground cardamom
- Salt to taste

Method:

1. Put onion, garlic, cilantro and parsley in a food processor.
2. Pulse until well combined.
3. Add the rest of the ingredients to the food processor.
4. Pulse until consistency is rough and coarse.
5. Put the mixture into a bowl.
6. Cover with foil and refrigerate for 1 hour.
7. Form into patties.
8. Preheat your air fryer to 400 degrees F.
9. Spray air fryer basket with oil.
10. Put the patties in the air fryer basket and cook for 10 minutes.
11. Cook in batches.

Nutritional Value:

- Calories 150
- Total Fat 2.5 g
- Saturated Fat 0 g
- Cholesterol 0 mg

- Sodium 160 mg
- Total Carbohydrate 25 g
- Dietary Fiber 7 g

- Total Sugars 4 g
- Protein 8 g
- Potassium 560 mg

Lentil Balls with Rice

Preparation Time: 10 minutes
Cooking Time: 20 minutes
Servings: 4

Ingredients:

- 30 oz. lentils, rinsed and drained
- 3 tablespoons mushrooms, chopped
- 1 cup walnuts, sliced in half
- 3 tablespoons fresh parsley, chopped
- 1 ½ tablespoons tomato paste
- Salt and pepper to taste
- ½ cup breadcrumbs
- 4 cups cooked rice
- 2 tablespoons lemon juice
- 2 teaspoons lemon zest
- 1 ½ tablespoons fresh parsley, minced
- 2 cups lettuce, chopped
- 1 cup cherry tomatoes, sliced in half
- ¼ cup onion, chopped
- 4 lemon wedges

Method:

1. Put the lentils, mushrooms, walnuts, 3 tablespoons parsley, tomato paste, salt and pepper in a food processor.
2. Pulse until chopped into smaller pieces.
3. Add the breadcrumbs and pulse for a few seconds until well combined.
4. Form balls from the mixture.
5. Cook the lentil balls in the air fryer at 380 degrees F for 10 minutes.
6. In a pan over medium heat, add the cooked rice.
7. Add the lemon juice, lemon zest and remaining parsley.
8. Cook for 5 minutes, stirring frequently.

9. Divide the rice into 4 bowls.
10. Top with the lentil's balls, lettuce, tomato, onion and lemon wedges.

Nutritional Value:

- Calories 659
- Total Fat 20 g
- Saturated Fat 2 g
- Cholesterol 1 mg
- Sodium 583 mg

- Total Carbohydrate 101 g
- Dietary Fiber 15 g
- Total Sugars 6 g
- Protein 23 g
- Potassium 1061 mg

Sweet & Spicy Cauliflower

Preparation Time: 10 minutes
Cooking Time: 30 minutes
Servings: 4

Ingredients:

- 4 cups cauliflower florets
- 1 onion, chopped
- 5 cloves garlic, chopped
- 1 ½ tablespoons tamari
- 1 tablespoon rice vinegar
- ½ teaspoon coconut sugar
- 1 tablespoon hot sauce
- 2 scallions, chopped

Method:

1. Put the cauliflower in the air fryer basket.
2. Cook at 350 degrees F for 10 minutes, shaking halfway through.
3. Add the onion and cook for another 10 minutes.
4. Add the garlic and stir.
5. Cook for 5 more minutes.
6. In a bowl, mix all the ingredients except the scallions.
7. Add to the air fryer. Mix well.
8. Cook for 5 minutes.
9. Sprinkle scallions on top before serving.

Nutritional Value:

- Calories 93
- Total Fat 3 g
- Saturated Fat 1 g
- Cholesterol 2 mg
- Sodium 510 mg
- Total Carbohydrate 12 g
- Dietary Fiber 3 g
- Total Sugars 4 g
- Protein 4 g
- Potassium 519 mg

Eggplant Parmesan

Preparation Time: 10 minutes
Cooking Time: 20 minutes
Servings: 6
Ingredients:

- 2 tablespoons vegan Parmesan cheese, grated
- ½ cup breadcrumbs
- Garlic powder to taste
- Onion powder to taste
- Salt and pepper to taste
- 1 eggplant, sliced
- ½ cup flour
- ½ cup almond milk
- Cooking spray
- 1 cup marinara sauce
- ½ cup vegan mozzarella, shredded
- Parsley, chopped

Method:

1. In a bowl, mix the Parmesan cheese, breadcrumbs, garlic powder, onion powder, salt and pepper.
2. Dip each eggplant slice in flour, then dip into the almond milk and then cover with Parmesan and breadcrumb mixture.
3. Spray air fryer basket with oil.
4. Cook the eggplant in the air fryer at 390 degrees F for 15 minutes, flipping halfway through.
5. Top with marinara sauce, mozzarella and parsley before serving.

Nutritional Value:

- Calories 176
- Total Fat 6.7g
- Saturated Fat 4.7g
- Cholesterol 1mg
- Sodium 242mg
- Total Carbohydrate 25.9g
- Dietary Fiber 4.9g
- Total Sugars 7.3g
- Protein 4.3g
- Potassium 389mg

Mushroom & Green Bean Casserole

Preparation Time: 10 minutes
Cooking Time: 10 minutes
Servings: 6

Ingredients:

- 24 oz. green beans, trimmed
- 2 cups button mushrooms, sliced
- 1 tablespoon lemon juice
- 1 tablespoon garlic powder
- ¾ teaspoon ground sage
- 1 teaspoon onion powder
- Salt and pepper to taste
- Cooking spray

Method:

1. Combine all the ingredients in a bowl.
2. Transfer to the air fryer basket and coat with oil.
3. Cook at 400 degrees F for 12 minutes.
4. Shake every 3 minutes.

Nutritional Value:

- Calories 47
- Total Fat 0.3g
- Saturated Fat 0.1g
- Cholesterol 0mg
- Sodium 9mg
- Total Carbohydrate 10.3g
- Dietary Fiber 4.3g
- Total Sugars 2.5g
- Protein 3.1g
- Potassium 335mg

"Crab" Cake

Preparation Time: 20 minutes
Cooking Time: 15 minutes
Servings: 8

Ingredients:

- 5 potatoes, diced
- 2 stalks green onion, chopped
- 1 teaspoon lemon juice
- ½ teaspoon lemon zest
- 1 teaspoon ginger, grated
- 1 tablespoon soy sauce
- 4 tablespoons red curry paste
- Salt and pepper to taste
- Cooking spray

Method:

1. Put all the ingredients in a food processor.
2. Pulse until tender and well combined.
3. Drain and then form into patties.
4. Spray air fryer basket with oil.
5. Cook at 400 degrees F for 20 to 25 minutes until fully cooked. Flip halfway through the cooking.

Nutritional Value:

- Calories 97
- Total Fat 1 g
- Saturated Fat 0.4 g
- Cholesterol 0 mg
- Sodium 580 mg
- Total Carbohydrate 25 g
- Dietary Fiber 5 g
- Total Sugars 2 g
- Protein 4 g
- Potassium 550 mg

Cauliflower Steak

Preparation Time: 5 minutes
Cooking Time: 15 minutes
Servings: 6

Ingredients:

- 2 heads cauliflower, green leaves removed, sliced into thick "steaks"
- 2 tablespoons coconut oil
- Salt and pepper to taste
- ¼ teaspoon ground ginger
- 1 teaspoon ground turmeric
- Tahini
- Sesame seeds
- Steamed green beans

Method:

1. Coat the cauliflower steaks with oil and season with salt, pepper, ginger and turmeric.
2. Place in the air fryer and cook at 390 degrees F for 15 minutes. Flip halfway through.
3. Drizzle with tahini and sesame seeds.
4. Serve with green beans.

Nutritional Value:

- Calories 66
- Total Fat 4.7g
- Saturated Fat 3.9g
- Cholesterol 0mg
- Sodium 27mg

- Total Carbohydrate 5.6g
- Dietary Fiber 2.6g
- Total Sugars 2.3g
- Protein 2g
- Potassium 297mg

Tofu Buddha Bowl

Preparation Time: 15 minutes
Cooking Time: 35 minutes
Servings: 6

Ingredients:

- ¼ cup soy sauce
- 2 tablespoons sesame oil
- 2 tablespoons lime juice
- 1 tablespoon hot sauce
- 3 tablespoons molasses
- 14 oz. tofu, cubed
- Cooking spray
- 1 lb. fresh broccoli florets
- 1 red bell pepper, sliced thinly
- 3 carrots, sliced thinly
- 8 oz. fresh spinach
- 1 teaspoon garlic, minced
- 1 tablespoon olive oil
- 2 cups cooked quinoa

Method:

1. In a bowl, mix the soy sauce, oil, lime juice, hot sauce and molasses.
2. Marinate tofu for 10 minutes.
3. Spray air fryer basket with oil.
4. Cook tofu in the air fryer at 370 degrees F for 15 minutes. Shake every 5 minutes.
5. Add broccoli, bell pepper and carrots in the marinade.
6. Marinate for 10 minutes.
7. In a pan over medium heat, sauté the garlic in olive oil and add the spinach.
8. Cook until the spinach has wilted but do not overcook.
9. Cook the marinated vegetables in the air fryer for 10 minutes, shaking once or twice halfway through.

10. In a serving bowl, put the quinoa and then arrange the tofu, vegetables and spinach.

Nutritional Value:

- Calories 236
- Total Fat 8 g
- Saturated Fat 2 g
- Cholesterol 5 mg
- Sodium 731 mg
- Total Carbohydrate 31 g
- Dietary Fiber 6 g
- Total Sugars 11 g
- Protein 12 g
- Potassium 926 mg

Seitan Riblets

Preparation Time: 15 minutes
Cooking Time: 20 minutes
Servings: 4

Ingredients:

- ¼ cup nutritional yeast
- 1 cup vital wheat gluten
- 1 teaspoon onion powder
- 1 teaspoon mushroom powder
- ½ teaspoon garlic powder
- Salt to taste
- ¼ cup barbecue sauce

Method:

1. Add all the ingredients except water and barbecue sauce in the food processor.
2. Pulse until smooth.
3. Knead the dough with your hands and form a round or square shape.
4. Place the seitan pieces in the air fryer.
5. Cook at 370 degrees F for 8 minutes.
6. Flip and then cook for another 5 minutes.
7. Drizzle with barbecue sauce before serving.

Nutritional Value:

- Calories 93
- Total Fat 0.7g
- Saturated Fat 0.1g
- Cholesterol 0mg
- Sodium 222mg
- Total Carbohydrate 12.7g
- Dietary Fiber 2.7g
- Total Sugars 4.4g
- Protein 10.5g
- Potassium 282mg

Italian Tofu

Preparation Time: 10 minutes
Cooking Time: 10 minutes
Servings: 2

Ingredients:

- 8 oz. tofu, sliced lengthwise
- 1 tablespoon tamari
- 1 tablespoon broth
- ½ teaspoon dried oregano
- ½ teaspoon dried basil
- ½ teaspoon granulated garlic
- ¼ teaspoon granulated onion
- Pepper to taste

Method:

1. Drain the tofu slices with paper towel.
2. Mix the rest of the ingredients in a bowl.
3. Coat the tofu with the mixture and marinate for 10 minutes.
4. Preheat your air fryer to 400 degrees F.
5. Cook the tofu in the air fryer for 6 minutes.
6. Flip and then cook for another 4 minutes.
7. Serve with pasta or vegetables.

Nutritional Value:

- Calories 87
- Total Fat 4.4 g
- Saturated Fat 1 g
- Cholesterol 0 mg
- Sodium 452 mg
- Total Carbohydrate 3.4 g
- Dietary Fiber 1.3 g
- Total Sugars 1 g
- Protein 10 g
- Potassium 221 mg

Barbecue Soy Curls

Preparation Time: 13 minutes
Cooking Time: 8 minutes
Servings: 2

Ingredients:

- 1 cup soy curls
- 1 cup warm water
- 1 teaspoon vegan bouillon
- ¼ cup barbecue sauce

Method:

1. Soak the soy curls in water and bouillon for 10 minutes.
2. Drain and squeeze out excess water.
3. Shred soy curls.
4. Cook in the air fryer at 400 degrees F for 3 minutes.
5. Toss in barbecue sauce and then put back in the air fryer.
6. Cook for another 5 minutes, shaking the basket twice.

Nutritional Value:

- Calories 136
- Total Fat 3 g
- Saturated Fat 1 g
- Cholesterol 5 mg
- Sodium 552 mg
- Total Carbohydrate 18 g
- Dietary Fiber 2 g
- Total Sugars 12 g
- Protein 7 g
- Potassium 160 mg

Chapter 7: Vegetable and Sides Recipes

French Fries

Preparation Time: 40 minutes
Cooking Time: 30 minutes
Servings: 3

Ingredients:

- 2 potatoes, sliced into thick strips
- 1 bowl water
- 2 tablespoons olive oil
- Salt and pepper to taste
- ¼ teaspoon paprika
- 1 tablespoon cornstarch
- Cooking spray
- Green onion, chopped

Method:

1. Soak potato strips in water for 30 minutes.
2. Drain and pat try.
3. Toss in olive oil.
4. Season with salt, pepper and paprika.
5. Cover with cornstarch.
6. Spray air fryer basket with oil.
7. Cook at 360 degrees F for 30 minutes shaking every 5 minutes.
8. Garnish with green onion.

Nutritional Value:

- Calories 185
- Total Fat 9 g
- Saturated Fat 1 g
- Cholesterol 0 mg
- Sodium 297 mg
- Total Carbohydrate 23 g
- Dietary Fiber 2 g
- Total Sugars 1 g
- Protein 2 g
- Potassium 482 mg

Crispy Zucchini Wedges

Preparation Time: 10 minutes
Cooking Time: 12 minutes
Servings: 6

Ingredients:

- Cooking spray
- ½ cup all-purpose flour
- 2 vegan eggs
- 2 tablespoons water
- 1 ½ breadcrumbs
- 1 zucchini, sliced into wedges
- ½ tablespoon red-wine vinegar
- 2 tablespoons tomato paste
- Salt and pepper to taste

Method:

1. Spray air fryer basket with oil.
2. Put the flour in a dish.
3. In another dish, combine vegan eggs and water.
4. In a third dish, put the breadcrumbs.
5. Dip each zucchini strip into the three dishes, first the flour, then the eggs and water, and lastly the breadcrumbs.
6. Cook in the air fryer at 360 degrees F for 12 minutes, shaking once.
7. Mix the rest of the ingredients in a bowl.
8. Serve zucchini fries with dipping sauce.

Nutritional Value:

- Calories 235
- Total Fat 12 g
- Saturated Fat 1 g
- Cholesterol 66 mg
- Sodium 232 mg
- Total Carbohydrate 26 g
- Dietary Fiber 2 g
- Total Sugars 2 g
- Protein 6 g
- Potassium 435 mg

Sweet Potato Chips

Preparation Time: 40 minutes
Cooking Time: 15 minutes
Servings: 4

Ingredients:

- 1 sweet potato, sliced into thin rounds
- 1 bowl water
- 1 tablespoon olive oil
- Salt and pepper to taste
- Cooking spray

Method:

1. Soak sweet potato slices in a bowl of water for 30 minutes.
2. Drain and then dry with paper towels.
3. Toss in oil and season with salt and pepper.
4. Spray air fryer basket with oil.
5. Cook sweet potato at 350 degrees F for 15 minutes, shaking every 5 minutes.

Nutritional Value:

- Calories 62
- Total Fat 4 g
- Saturated Fat 1 g
- Cholesterol 10 mg
- Sodium 169 mg
- Total Carbohydrate 14 g
- Dietary Fiber 1 g
- Total Sugars 1 g
- Protein 0 g
- Potassium 160 mg

Baked Potatoes with Broccoli & Cheese

Preparation Time: 10 minutes
Cooking Time: 30 minutes
Servings: 8

Ingredients:

- 4 potatoes
- 1 cup almond milk, divided
- 2 tablespoons all-purpose flour
- ½ cup vegan cheese, divided
- 1 cup broccoli, florets, chopped
- Salt to taste
- Chopped onion chives

Method:

1. Poke all sides of potatoes with a fork.
2. Microwave on high level for 5 minutes.
3. Flip and microwave for another 5 minutes.
4. In a saucepan over medium heat, heat ¾ cup of milk for 2 minutes, stirring frequently.
5. Add the remaining milk in a bowl and stir in the flour.
6. Add this mixture to the pan and bring to a boil.
7. Reduce heat
8. Reserve 2 tablespoons vegan cheese.
9. Add the rest of the cheese to the pan and stir until smooth.
10. Add the broccoli, salt and cayenne.
11. Cook for 1 minute and remove from heat.
12. Slice the potatoes and arrange on a single layer inside the air fryer.
13. Top with the broccoli mixture.
14. Add another layer of potatoes and broccoli mixture.
15. Sprinkle reserved cheese on top.
16. Cook at 350 degrees F for 5 minutes.
17. Garnish with chopped chives.

Nutritional Value:

- Calories 137
- Total Fat 3 g
- Saturated Fat 2 g
- Cholesterol 9 mg
- Sodium 112 mg

- Total Carbohydrate 148 g
- Dietary Fiber 2 g
- Total Sugars 3 g
- Protein 5 g
- Potassium 556 mg

Kale Chips

Preparation Time: 5 minutes
Cooking Time: 10 minutes
Servings: 2

Ingredients:

- Cooking spray
- 6 cups kale leaves, torn
- 1 tablespoon olive oil
- Salt to taste
- 1 ½ teaspoons low-sodium soy sauce
- ¼ teaspoon ground cumin
- ½ teaspoon white sesame seeds

Method:

1. Spray air fryer basket with oil.
2. Toss kale in oil, salt and soy sauce.
3. Cook at 375 degrees F for 10 minutes or until crispy. Shake every 3 minutes.
4. Sprinkle with cumin and sesame seeds before serving.

Nutritional Value:

- Calories 140
- Total Fat 9 g
- Saturated Fat 1 g
- Cholesterol 0 mg
- Sodium 329 mg
- Total Carbohydrate 13 g
- Dietary Fiber 4 g
- Total Sugars 3 g
- Protein 4 g
- Potassium 497 mg

Garlic Mushrooms

Preparation Time: 10 minutes
Cooking Time: 15 minutes
Servings: 2

Ingredients:

- 8 oz. mushrooms, rinsed, dried and sliced in half
- 1 tablespoon olive oil
- ½ teaspoon garlic powder
- Salt and pepper to taste
- 1 teaspoon Worcestershire sauce
- 1 tablespoon parsley, chopped

Method:

1. Toss mushrooms in oil.
2. Season with garlic powder, salt, pepper and Worcestershire sauce.
3. Cook at 380 degrees F for 10 minutes, shaking halfway through.
4. Top with parsley before serving.

Nutritional Value:

- Calories 90
- Total Fat 7.4g
- Saturated Fat 1g
- Cholesterol 0mg
- Sodium 35mg
- Total Carbohydrate 4.9g
- Dietary Fiber 1.3g
- Total Sugars 2.6g
- Protein 3.8g
- Potassium 379mg

Rosemary Potatoes

Preparation Time: 15 minutes
Cooking Time: 15 minutes
Servings: 4

Ingredients:

- 4 potatoes, cubed
- 1 tablespoon oil
- 1 tablespoon garlic, minced
- 2 teaspoons dried rosemary, minced
- Salt and pepper to taste
- 1 tablespoon lime juice
- ¼ cup parsley, chopped

Method:

1. Toss potato cubes in oil and season with garlic, rosemary, salt and pepper.
2. Put in the air fryer.
3. Cook at 400 degrees F for 15 minutes.
4. Stir in lime juice and top with parsley before serving.

Nutritional Value:

- Calories 244
- Total Fat 10.5g
- Saturated Fat 2.1g
- Cholesterol 0mg
- Sodium 16mg
- Total Carbohydrate 35g
- Dietary Fiber 5.6g
- Total Sugars 2.6g
- Protein 3.9g
- Potassium 905mg

Roasted Spicy Carrots

Preparation Time: 5 minutes
Cooking Time: 15 minutes
Servings: 4

Ingredients:

- ½ lb. carrots, sliced
- ½ tablespoon olive oil
- Salt to taste
- 1/8 teaspoon garlic powder
- ¼ teaspoon chili powder
- 1 teaspoon ground cumin
- Sesame seeds
- Fresh cilantro

Method:

1. Preheat your air fryer at 390 degrees F for 5 minutes.
2. Cook the carrots at 390 degrees F for 10 minutes.
3. Transfer to a bowl.
4. Mix the oil, salt, garlic powder, chili powder and ground cumin.
5. Coat the carrots with the oil mixture.
6. Put the carrots back to the air fryer and cook for another 5 minutes.
7. Garnish with sesame seeds and cilantro.

Nutritional Value:

- Calories 82
- Total Fat 3.8g
- Saturated Fat 0.5g
- Cholesterol 0mg
- Sodium 161mg
- Total Carbohydrate 11.9g
- Dietary Fiber 3g
- Total Sugars 5.7g
- Protein 1.2g
- Potassium 390mg

Baked Artichoke Fries

Preparation Time: 10 minutes
Cooking Time: 10 minutes
Servings: 4

Ingredients:

- 14 oz. canned artichoke hearts, drained, rinsed and sliced into wedges
- 1 cup all-purpose flour
- ½ cup almond milk
- ½ teaspoon garlic powder
- Salt and pepper to taste
- 1 ½ cup breadcrumbs
- ½ teaspoon paprika

Method:

1. Dry the artichoke hearts by pressing a paper towel on top.
2. In a bowl, mix the flour, milk, garlic powder, salt and pepper.
3. In a shallow dish, add the paprika and breadcrumbs.
4. Dip each artichoke wedge in the first bowl and then coat with the breadcrumb mixture.
5. Cook at 450 degrees for 10 minutes.
6. Serve fries with your choice of dipping sauce.

Nutritional Value:

- Calories 391
- Total Fat 9.8g
- Saturated Fat 6.9g
- Cholesterol 0mg
- Sodium 395mg
- Total Carbohydrate 65.5g
- Dietary Fiber 8.8g
- Total Sugars 4.7g
- Protein 12.7g
- Potassium 569mg

Baked Tofu Strips

Preparation Time: 30 minutes
Cooking Time: 40 minutes
Servings: 4

Ingredients:

- 2 tablespoons olive oil
- ½ teaspoon oregano
- ½ teaspoon basil
- ¼ teaspoon cayenne pepper
- ¼ teaspoon paprika
- ¼ teaspoon garlic powder
- ¼ teaspoon onion powder
- Salt and pepper to taste
- 15 oz. tofu, drained

Method:

1. Combine all the ingredients except the tofu.
2. Mix well.
3. Slice tofu into strips and dry with paper towel.
4. Marinate in the mixture for 10 minutes.
5. Cook in the air fryer at 375 degrees F for 15 minutes, shaking halfway through.

Nutritional Value:

- Calories 132
- Total Fat 10 g
- Saturated Fat 1 g
- Cholesterol 0 mg
- Sodium 40 mg
- Total Carbohydrate 3 g
- Dietary Fiber 0 g
- Total Sugars 1 g
- Protein 7 g
- Potassium 213 mg

Avocado Fries

Preparation Time: 10 minutes
Cooking Time: 10 minutes
Servings: 4

Ingredients:

- Salt to taste
- ½ cup panko breadcrumbs
- 1 cup aquafaba liquid
- 1 avocado, sliced into strips

Method:

1. Mix the salt and breadcrumbs in a bowl.
2. In another bowl, pour the aquafaba liquid.
3. Dip each avocado strip into the liquid and then dredge with breadcrumbs.
4. Air fry at 390 degrees F for 10 minutes, shaking halfway through.

Nutritional Value:

- Calories 111
- Total Fat 9.9g
- Saturated Fat 2.1g
- Cholesterol 0mg
- Sodium 59mg
- Total Carbohydrate 6.2g
- Dietary Fiber 3.6g
- Total Sugars 0.3g
- Protein 1.2g
- Potassium 244mg

Crispy Vegetables

Preparation Time: 15 minutes
Cooking Time: 8 minutes
Servings: 4

Ingredients:

- 1 cup rice flour
- 1 tablespoon nutritional yeast flakes
- 2 tablespoons vegan egg powder
- 2/3 cup cold water
- 1 cup breadcrumbs
- Salt and pepper to taste
- 1 cup squash, sliced into strips
- 1 cup zucchini, sliced into strips
- ½ cup green beans
- ½ cup cauliflower, sliced into florets
- Cooking spray

Method:

1. Set up three bowls.
2. One is for the rice flour, another for the egg powder, nutritional yeast and water, another for the breadcrumbs.
3. Dip each of the vegetable slices in the first, second and third bowls.
4. Spray the air fryer basket with oil.
5. Cook at 380 degrees F for 8 minutes or until crispy.

Nutritional Value:

- Calories 272
- Total Fat 2.2g
- Saturated Fat 0.5g
- Cholesterol 0mg
- Sodium 208mg
- Total Carbohydrate 54.8g
- Dietary Fiber 3.9g
- Total Sugars 2.7g
- Protein 7.9g
- Potassium 284mg

Chapter 8: Salad Recipes

Roasted Vegetable Salad

Preparation Time: 1 hour and 30 minutes
Cooking Time: 25 minutes
Servings: 6

Ingredients:

- 1 sweet potato, chopped
- 1 red bell pepper, chopped
- 1 onion, chopped
- 4 small potatoes, chopped
- ¼ cup cherry tomatoes, chopped
- Salt and pepper to taste
- ¼ cup parsley, chopped
- 2 tablespoons capers, chopped
- 1 avocado, chopped
- 1 tablespoon lemon juice
- 1 tablespoon olive oil
- 1 can chickpeas mixed with 1 teaspoon mustard powder
- 4 cups lettuce leaves, chopped

Method:

1. Season all the vegetables (except parsley, capers, lettuce and avocado) with salt and pepper.
2. Toss in oil and cook in the air fryer at 400 degrees for 25 minutes.
3. Transfer to a bowl and refrigerate for 1 hour.
4. Mash avocado and mix with lemon juice and olive oil.
5. Arrange the salad in a bowl by putting the lettuce leaves first and topping with the cooked vegetables and chickpeas.
6. Serve with the avocado dressing.

Nutritional Value:

- Calories 206
- Total Fat 9.2g
- Saturated Fat 1.8g
- Cholesterol 0mg
- Sodium 106mg

- Total Carbohydrate 29.6g
- Dietary Fiber 6.8g
- Total Sugars 5.1g
- Protein 3.7g
- Potassium 866mg

Vegetable & Pasta Salad

Preparation Time: 1 hour and 5 minutes
Cooking Time: 1 hour and 45 minutes
Servings: 4

Ingredients:

- 3 eggplants, sliced
- 2 tablespoons olive oil, divided
- Salt and pepper to taste
- 3 zucchinis, sliced
- 4 tomatoes, sliced into wedges
- 4 cups macaroni pasta
- Salt to taste
- 8 tablespoons vegan Parmesan cheese, grated
- ½ cup Italian dressing
- Basil leaves, chopped

Method:

1. Toss eggplant slices in 1 tablespoon olive oil and season with salt and pepper.
2. Cook in the air fryer at 375 degrees F for 40 minutes.
3. Toss the zucchini in the remaining oil and cook in the air fryer for 25 minutes.
4. Cook pasta according to the package directions. Drain and rinse.
5. Toss the pasta with the eggplant and zucchini slices.
6. Drizzle with Italian dressing.
7. Season with salt.
8. Sprinkle cheese and basil on top, and serve.

Nutritional Value:

- Calories 336
- Total Fat 11.7g
- Saturated Fat 1.6g
- Cholesterol 13mg
- Sodium 52mg
- Total Carbohydrate 52g
- Dietary Fiber 13.1g
- Total Sugars 15g
- Protein 9.3g
- Potassium 1158mg

Crispy Tofu & Avocado Salad

Preparation Time: 15 minutes
Cooking Time: 15 minutes
Servings: 6

Ingredients:

- Cooking spray
- 2 cups tofu, cubed
- 4 cups mixed greens
- 4 cups Romaine lettuce
- ½ cup onion, sliced
- 1 cup cherry tomatoes, sliced in half
- ½ avocado, sliced into cubes
- ½ cup red wine vinegar
- 1 cup avocado lime dressing

Method:

1. Spray air fryer basket with oil.
2. Cook the tofu cubes at 375 degrees F for 15 minutes, shaking halfway through.
3. In a bowl, arrange the salad by topping the lettuce and mixed greens with crispy tofu, onion, tomatoes and avocado.
4. Drizzle with red wine vinegar and avocado lime dressing.

Nutritional Value:

- Calories 287
- Total Fat 10.8g
- Saturated Fat 2.2g
- Cholesterol 0mg
- Sodium 88mg
- Total Carbohydrate 33.1g
- Dietary Fiber 12g
- Total Sugars 9g
- Protein 16.8g
- Potassium 843mg

Radish & Mozzarella Salad

Preparation Time: 15 minutes
Cooking Time: 30 minutes
Servings: 4

Ingredients:

- 1 lb. radish, sliced into rounds
- 2 tablespoons olive oil
- Salt and pepper to taste
- ½ lb. vegan mozzarella, sliced into rounds
- 2 tablespoons balsamic glaze

Method:

1. Toss radish rounds in oil and season with salt and pepper.
2. Cook in the air fryer at 350 degrees F for 30 minutes, shaking once or twice during cooking.
3. Arrange on a serving platter with the vegan mozzarella.
4. Drizzle cheese and radish with balsamic glaze before serving.

Nutritional Value:

- Calories 88
- Total Fat 7.7g
- Saturated Fat 1.4g
- Cholesterol 2mg
- Sodium 65mg
- Total Carbohydrate 4g
- Dietary Fiber 1.8g
- Total Sugars 2.1g
- Protein 1.8g
- Potassium 265mg

Roasted Butternut Squash Salad

Preparation Time: 10 minutes
Cooking Time: 15 minutes
Servings: 4

Ingredients:

- 1 butternut squash, sliced into cubes
- 4 tablespoons olive oil, divided
- ¼ teaspoon cayenne pepper
- Salt to taste
- 2 tablespoons fresh lemon juice
- 1 shallot, minced
- 6 oz. arugula
- 1 apple, sliced thinly
- ½ cup almonds, toasted and sliced
- ½ cup vegan Parmesan cheese, grated

Method:

1. Toss squash cubes in 1 tablespoon olive oil and cayenne pepper.
2. Add to the air fryer and cook at 400 degrees F for 15 minutes, shaking once or twice.
3. In a bowl, mix the salt, remaining olive oil, lemon juice and shallot.
4. Coat arugula with this mixture.
5. Arrange arugula on salad bowls.
6. Top with the squash cubes, apple slices, almonds and Parmesan cheese.

Nutritional Value:

- Calories 295
- Total Fat 20.5g
- Saturated Fat 2.6g
- Cholesterol 0mg
- Sodium 58mg
- Total Carbohydrate 28.8g
- Dietary Fiber 6.4g
- Total Sugars 10.4g
- Protein 5.3g
- Potassium 816mg

Green Salad with Roasted Bell Peppers

Preparation Time: 10 minutes
Cooking Time: 10 minutes
Servings: 4

Ingredients:

- 1 red bell pepper
- 1 tablespoon lemon juice
- 2 tablespoons olive oil
- 3 tablespoons vegan yogurt
- Pepper to taste
- 4 cups Romaine lettuce, chopped

Method:

1. Preheat your air fryer to 400 degrees F.
2. Add the bell pepper inside.
3. Cook for 10 minutes or until slightly charred.
4. Slice the roasted bell peppers.
5. Top the Romaine lettuce with the roasted bell peppers.
6. In a bowl, mix the rest of the ingredients and serve as dressing.

Nutritional Value:

- Calories 205
- Total Fat 14g
- Saturated Fat 1g
- Cholesterol 0mg
- Sodium 12mg
- Total Carbohydrate 18.3g
- Dietary Fiber 0.8g
- Total Sugars 9.6g
- Protein 3.6g
- Potassium 139mg

Salad Topped with Garlic Croutons

Preparation Time: 10 minutes
Cooking Time: 5 minutes
Servings: 4

Ingredients:

- 4 slices vegan bread, sliced into cubes
- 1 tablespoon olive oil
- Garlic powder to taste
- Salt and pepper to taste
- 1 teaspoon Italian seasoning
- Mixed greens
- 1 cup tomato, chopped
- 1 cup white onion rings

Method:

1. Coat the bread cubes with olive oil.
2. Season with garlic powder, salt, pepper and Italian seasoning.
3. Cook in the air fryer at 380 degrees F for 5 minutes, shaking a few times.
4. Place the mixed greens in a bowl,
5. Top with the tomato, white onions and croutons.
6. Serve with vegan salad dressing.

Nutritional Value:

- Calories 50
- Total Fat 4.1g
- Saturated Fat 0.6g
- Cholesterol 1mg
- Sodium 13mg
- Total Carbohydrate 4g
- Dietary Fiber 0.6g
- Total Sugars 1.3g
- Protein 0.4g
- Potassium 109mg

Green Bean Salad

Preparation Time: 35 minutes
Cooking Time: 15 minutes
Servings: 2

Ingredients:

- 2 cups green beans, trimmed
- ¼ cup water
- ¼ cup vegan mayo
- ¼ cup vegan cheese

Method:

1. Put the green beans and water in a small heatproof pan.
2. Put the pan in the air fryer basket.
3. Cook in the air fryer at 375 degrees F for 15 minutes.
4. Let cool.
5. Put in the refrigerator for 30 minutes.
6. Mix with mayo and top with cheese.

Nutritional Value:

- Calories 97
- Total Fat 6.1g
- Saturated Fat 0.5g
- Cholesterol 0mg
- Sodium 203mg
- Total Carbohydrate 10.1g
- Dietary Fiber 3.9g
- Total Sugars 1.5g
- Protein 2g
- Potassium 230mg

Salad with Roasted Tomatoes

Preparation Time: 5 minutes
Cooking Time: 45 minutes
Servings: 4

Ingredients:

- 2 cups tomatoes, sliced
- Salt to taste
- 4 cups Romaine lettuce leaves
- 2 cups arugula
- 1 cup onion, chopped
- Vegan salad dressing

Method:

1. Toss tomato slices in olive oil.
2. Season with salt.
3. Cook in the air fryer at 240 degrees F for 45 minutes.
4. Arrange lettuce and arugula on salad bowls.
5. Top with onion and roasted tomatoes.
6. Serve with vegan salad dressing.

Nutritional Value:

- Calories 73
- Total Fat 3.9g
- Saturated Fat 0.4g
- Cholesterol 0mg
- Sodium 85mg
- Total Carbohydrate 8.7g
- Dietary Fiber 2.2g
- Total Sugars 4.6g
- Protein 1.6g
- Potassium 370mg

Mixed Greens with Corn

Preparation Time: 15 minutes
Cooking Time: 10 minutes
Servings: 2

Ingredients:

- 3 ears corn
- Cooking spray
- Salt and pepper to taste
- 3 cups mixed greens
- 1 cup cucumber, sliced into small cubes
- 1 cup tomatoes, chopped
- Vegan salad dressing

Method:

1. Preheat your air fryer to 400 degrees F.
2. Spray corn with oil.
3. Season with salt and pepper.
4. Cook in the air fryer for 10 minutes, flipping halfway through.
5. Remove from heat and slice to get the kernels.
6. Put mixed greens in salad bowls.
7. Top with cucumber, tomatoes and corn kernels.
8. Serve with the dressing.

Nutritional Value:

- Calories 157
- Total Fat 3.5g
- Saturated Fat 0.5g
- Cholesterol 0mg
- Sodium 69mg
- Total Carbohydrate 28.6g
- Dietary Fiber 6.6g
- Total Sugars 6.6g
- Protein 5.5g
- Potassium 459mg

Chapter 9: Dessert Recipes

Apple Chips

Preparation Time: 10 minutes
Cooking Time: 20 minutes
Servings: 2

Ingredients:

- 1 apple, sliced thinly
- Salt to taste
- ¼ teaspoon ground cinnamon

Method:

1. Preheat the air fryer to 350 degrees F.
2. Toss the apple slices in salt and cinnamon.
3. Add to the air fryer.
4. Let cool before serving.

Nutritional Value:

- Calories 59
- Total Fat 0.2g
- Saturated Fat 0g
- Cholesterol 0mg
- Sodium 79mg
- Total Carbohydrate 15.6g
- Dietary Fiber 2.9g
- Total Sugars 11.6g
- Protein 0.3g
- Potassium 121mg

Fruit Crumble

Preparation Time: 10 minutes
Cooking Time: 15 minutes
Servings: 4

Ingredients:

- 1 apple, diced
- ¼ cup frozen blueberries
- ¼ cup frozen strawberries
- ¼ cup and 1 tablespoon brown rice flour
- 2 tablespoons sugar
- ½ teaspoon ground cinnamon
- 2 tablespoons vegan butter

Method:

1. Preheat your air fryer to 350 degrees F.
2. In a ramekin, combine the apple, blueberries and strawberries.
3. In another bowl, mix the rest of the ingredients.
4. Serve this mixture over the fruit mix.
5. Cook at 350 degrees F for 15 minutes.

Nutritional Value:

- Calories 310
- Total Fat 12 g
- Saturated Fat 7 g
- Cholesterol 31 mg
- Sodium 5 mg
- Total Carbohydrate 50 g
- Dietary Fiber 5 g
- Total Sugars 26 g
- Protein 2 g
- Potassium 557 mg

Fruit Kebab

Preparation Time: 30 minutes
Cooking Time: 6 minutes
Servings: 10

Ingredients:

- 1 teaspoon maple syrup
- 1 teaspoon lemon juice
- 1 apple, diced
- 1 mango, diced
- 1 pear, diced
- Salt to taste
- Lemon zest

Method:

1. In a bowl, combine maple syrup and lemon juice.
2. Coat the fruit cubes with the mixture.
3. Season with salt.
4. Arrange in skewers.
5. Place the skewers inside the air fryer and cook at 360 degrees for 5 minutes.
6. Garnish with lemon zest.

Nutritional Value:

- Calories 52
- Total Fat 0.2g
- Saturated Fat 0.1g
- Cholesterol 0mg
- Sodium 20mg
- Total Carbohydrate 13.4g
- Dietary Fiber 1.9g
- Total Sugars 10.8g
- Protein 0.5g
- Potassium 123mg

Baked Apples with Pumpkin Spice

Preparation Time: 10 minutes
Cooking Time: 15 minutes
Servings: 4

Ingredients:

- 4 apples, sliced
- ¼ cup maple syrup
- ¼ cup rolled oats
- ¼ cup pecans, chopped
- 2 tablespoons raisins
- 1 teaspoon pumpkin spice seasoning
- 2/3 cup water

Method:

1. Coat apple slices with maple syrup and mix with oats, pecans and raisins.
2. Season with pumpkin spice.
3. Transfer the mixture into a small heatproof dish that can fit inside the air fryer.
4. In the air fryer, add the water.
5. Put the dish inside.
6. Cook at 340 degrees F for 15 minutes.

Nutritional Value:

- Calories 206
- Total Fat 1.4g
- Saturated Fat 0.1g
- Cholesterol 0mg
- Sodium 6mg
- Total Carbohydrate 51.2g
- Dietary Fiber 6.2g
- Total Sugars 37.7g
- Protein 1.5g
- Potassium 335mg

Vegan Brownies

Preparation Time: 15 minutes
Cooking Time: 20 minutes
Servings: 4

Ingredients:

- ½ cup whole wheat pastry flour
- ¼ cup cocoa powder
- ½ cup sugar
- 1 tablespoon ground flax seeds
- ¼ teaspoon salt
- ¼ cup almond milk
- ¼ cup aquafaba
- ½ teaspoon vanilla extract
- Chopped walnuts
- Cooking spray

Method:

1. Combine first five ingredients in a bowl.
2. Mix the rest of the ingredients except the walnuts in another bowl.
3. Slowly combine the two bowls.
4. Preheat your air fryer to 350 degrees F.
5. Spray air fryer with oil.
6. Pour the mixture into a heatproof pan.
7. Sprinkle top with walnuts.
8. Cook in the air fryer for 20 minutes.

Nutritional Value:

- Calories 206
- Total Fat 5.1g
- Saturated Fat 3.7g
- Cholesterol 0mg
- Sodium 151mg
- Total Carbohydrate 40.4g
- Dietary Fiber 3.9g
- Total Sugars 25.7g
- Protein 3.1g
- Potassium 189mg

Berry Crumble

Preparation Time: 15 minutes
Cooking Time: 12 minutes
Servings: 4

Ingredients:

- ½ cup blackberries
- ½ cup strawberries
- 1 cup blueberries
- ¼ cup flour
- ¼ cup sugar
- 1 teaspoon vanilla
- ½ cup quick oats
- ¼ cup brown sugar
- 1 teaspoon lemon juice
- 3 tablespoons melted butter

Method:

1. In a bowl, combine the berries, lemon juice and sugar.
2. In another bowl, mix the rest of the ingredients.
3. Toss the berries in the mixture.
4. Spray air fryer with oil.
5. Cook at 390 degrees F for 12 minutes.

Nutritional Value:

- Calories 262
- Total Fat 9.7g
- Saturated Fat 5.6g
- Cholesterol 23mg
- Sodium 66mg
- Total Carbohydrate 42.8g
- Dietary Fiber 3.4g
- Total Sugars 26.9g
- Protein 2.9g
- Potassium 148mg

Sweetened Plantains

Preparation Time: 5 minutes
Cooking Time: 8 minutes
Servings: 4

Ingredients:

- 2 ripe plantains, sliced
- 2 teaspoons avocado oil
- Salt to taste
- Maple syrup

Method:

1. Toss the plantains in oil.
2. Season with salt.
3. Cook in the air fryer basket at 400 degrees F for 10 minutes, shaking after 5 minutes.
4. Drizzle with maple syrup before serving.

Nutritional Value:

- Calories 125
- Total Fat 0.6g
- Saturated Fat 0.2g
- Cholesterol 0mg
- Sodium 43mg
- Total Carbohydrate 32g
- Dietary Fiber 2.2g
- Total Sugars 16.4g
- Protein 1.2g
- Potassium 464mg

Carrot Cake

Preparation Time: 10 minutes
Cooking Time: 15 minutes
Serving: 1

Ingredients:

- Cooking spray
- ¼ cups whole wheat pastry flour
- ¼ teaspoon baking powder
- 1 tablespoon coconut sugar
- 1/8 teaspoon ground dried ginger
- ¼ teaspoon ground cinnamon
- Salt to taste
- 2 tablespoons almond milk
- 2 teaspoons oil
- 2 tablespoons carrot, grated
- 1 tablespoons date, chopped
- 2 tablespoons walnuts, chopped
- Water

Method:

1. Spray a heatproof mug with oil.
2. In a bowl, mix the flour, baking powder, sugar, ginger, cinnamon and salt.
3. Pour in the milk and oil.
4. Add the carrot, dates and walnuts.
5. Mix well.
6. Put the mug inside the air fryer.
7. Pour water around it.
8. Cook in the air fryer at 350 degrees for 15 minutes or until middle part is fully cooked.

Nutritional Value:

- Calories 365
- Total Fat 17.5g
- Saturated Fat 6.9g
- Cholesterol 0mg

- Sodium 171mg
- Total Carbohydrate 48g
- Dietary Fiber 6.3g

- Total Sugars 20.9g
- Protein 7.8g
- Potassium 406mg

Roasted Bananas

Preparation Time: 5 minutes
Cooking Time: 5 minutes
Servings: 2

Ingredients:

- 2 cups bananas, cubed
- 1 teaspoon avocado oil
- 1 tablespoon maple syrup
- 1 teaspoon brown sugar
- 1 cup almond milk

Method:

1. Coat the banana cubes with oil and maple syrup.
2. Sprinkle with brown sugar.
3. Cook in the air fryer at 375 degrees F for 5 minutes.
4. Drizzle milk on top of the bananas before serving.

Nutritional Value:

- Calories 107
- Total Fat 0.7g
- Saturated Fat 0.0g
- Cholesterol 0mg
- Sodium 1mg
- Total Carbohydrates 27g
- Dietary Fiber 3.1g
- Protein 1.3g
- Sugars 14g
- Potassium 422mg

Pear Crisp

Preparation Time: 10 minutes
Cooking Time: 25 minutes
Servings: 2

Ingredients:

- 1 cup flour
- 1 stick vegan butter
- 1 tablespoon cinnamon
- ½ cup sugar
- 2 pears, cubed

Method:

1. Mix flour and butter to form crumbly texture.
2. Add cinnamon and sugar.
3. Put the pears in the air fryer.
4. Pour and spread the mixture on top of the pears.
5. Cook at 350 degrees F for 25 minutes.

Nutritional Value:

- Calories 544
- Total Fat 0.9g
- Saturated Fat 0.1g
- Cholesterol 0mg
- Sodium 4mg
- Total Carbohydrate 132.3g
- Dietary Fiber 10g
- Total Sugars 70.6g
- Protein 7.4g
- Potassium 324mg

Conclusion

Becoming a vegan certainly has many benefits.

It's not easy at first but once you get used to it, you'll definitely reap its countless benefits, particularly for one's health.

It's good to know that there are modern appliances like the air fryer that can help make things easier for you when you make the transition.

Cheers to a healthier you! Good luck!

CPSIA information can be obtained
at www.ICGtesting.com
Printed in the USA
LVHW102130120821
695203LV00002B/4